Where Fear Fails

Bruce Michael Goeas

Printed in the United States of America

First Printing, 2017

ISBN 9781549945410

Contents

Introduction

Chapter 1: The Human Dynamics of Fear

Chapter 2: Fear and the Individual

Chapter 3: Fear and the Dysfunctional Team

Chapter 4: Fear and the Organization at Risk

Chapter 5: Fear as a Leadership Approach

Chapter 6: How Courage Triumphs

INTRODUCTION

There we sat in Radio City Music Hall, prepped for two days of presentations from some of the most powerful leaders in the world. It was September 23, 2008 and news of a total financial meltdown had started to spread across various media outlets.

I watched the World Business Forum participants grow increasingly nervous and panicked as each presenter shared their concerns about what was happening just five miles away on Wall Street. The fear was palpable!

And so, it began--just as it has throughout history. Fear struck, rumors became commonplace, politicians seized the opportunity for their own purposes, and opinions became fact. Once again, we were reminded of our basic atavistic nature. In preparation for our 'fight or flight' response blood moved from our brains into large muscle groups—great for running or fighting, not so much for thinking clearly. World leaders from every walk of life stopped thinking and engaged in some pretty interesting, albeit silly, behavior.

As the next five years unfolded the number of people who stopped looking for work increased to the highest level in over 25 years. The economy struggled to recover. Again, I was reminded of how fear fails us.

The Great Recession of 2008-2010 is just the most recent example of ***Where Fear Fails.***

This is a book for individuals, leaders, and their organizations limited by fear on a daily basis.

In Chapter 1, we will explore how people react to fear by discussing the dynamics of fear. This foundational chapter will explore our physiological coding and how it impacts fear in the digital world.

Chapter 2 looks at how individual success is limited by fear and provides some thoughts on how individuals and leaders might mitigate fear's impact. This chapter will explore three types of fear; Making a Bad Decision, Loss, and Judgement.

Chapter 3 explores how fear contributes to team dysfunction and provides tips for team leaders on developing a successful team. Fears addressed in this chapter include fear of Public Embarrassment, Being Wrong, and Being an Outlier.

How organizations are placed at risk due to fear is the focus of Chapter 4. Here we will explore the impact of fear of Attack, Extinction, and Loss impacting organizational performance, success, and longevity.

The fallacy of using fear as a leadership approach is explored in Chapter 5. This chapter will look at the short-lived impact of fear, responses to ultimatums, and apathy.

The final chapter, Chapter 6, explores How Courage Triumphs. Success stories at the individual, team, and organizations are presented.

Chapter 1

THE DYNAMICS OF FEAR

"This great Nation will endure as it has endured, will revive and will prosper. So, first of all, let me assert my firm belief that the only thing we have to fear is fear itself—nameless, unreasoning, unjustified terror which paralyses needed efforts to convert retreat into advance."

FDR's First Inaugural Address

MASKS, SCREAMS, AND LITTLE PEOPLE, OH MY!

As I sat down to write this book, and thought about reactions to fear and their lasting impact my black and white cocker spaniel, Maddie, came to mind.

We adopted Maddie shortly after she was weened. During the first six months, she approached her new world with reckless abandon. We even nicknamed her Braveheart. She would approach any person, dog, or object without fear.

Then came her first Halloween. This change to her environment did not go well. The very children she had greeted earlier that day were now yelling something about tricks and treats, carrying swords and sticks, and wearing masks.

Our Braveheart now sees 'little people' as scary and unpredictable. Ever since our girl takes flight any time she hears a child screaming or sees them approaching her. We have tried several different approaches and none of them seem to reduce her fear.

As the children grow and get taller she views them as 'big people' (i.e., adults) and approaches them without regard. However, the imprinting is strong and has not diminished over the nine years she has been with us. Unfortunate for Maddie and the children who so badly want to know her.

You may be thinking, this makes for a fun story but what does this have to do with people, teams, or organizations?

Great Question!

In the past 30 years, more than once I have seen an individual take a single data point (e.g., a fear-based reaction to giving a speech in front of a small group), extend it to all similar circumstances, and decide to never go through that experience again. They often make this decision even if it is career limiting.

Additionally, I have worked with teams who take one missed deadline or opportunity and extrapolate that experience to all future events that looked or felt similar (e.g., not competing in a sales opportunity because they did not win the business in a similar situation). Instead of doing a postmortem on the negative event and learning from the experience, fear of repeating the event results in leaving good money on the table.

And, there have been countless organizations who have fled a marketplace when they should have gotten creative. Others stubbornly fought to keep their old business model or product because they feared a needed change. In other scenarios companies have gone out of business because they feared the consequences of the very change that might have helped them remain a going concern.

Truth is that our atavistic design takes over when fear presents itself. And, it doesn't always serve us well.

ATAVISTIC FEAR RESPONSES

There is no doubt we homo sapiens have made great progress since the days of the Neanderthals. We can multi-task, adapt rapidly to new technologies, and travel from point A to point B to places and at speeds once beyond comprehension. All requiring us to use our brains when things get a bit scary or difficult or challenging.

Here's the rub. At our core, we still revert to the same physiological responses to fear as our ancestors (atavism). We are in essence still cavewomen and cavemen. Our physiological responses to fear have not changed for thousands of years.

The simple description is when we experience fear parts of the brain (amygdala and hypothalamus) activate glands. These glands then release hormones resulting in increased heart rate and blood pressure, heavy breathing, constriction of blood vessels in parts of the body, dilation of blood vessels for muscles, flushing, narrowing of vision, and freeing of metabolic energy sources for muscular action.

The physiological responses preparing us for 'fight or flight' were great for situations dealing with dinosaurs and other primitive threats. For our purposes here let's use a common definition for each:

Fight: In response to a threat one moves toward and confronts (attacks) the threat.

Flight: Leaving the location of a threat. Running or moving away to avoid engaging a threat.

The challenge is that these innate responses may be passé. In today's digital world one can't respond to a stressor by punching or even yelling at a co-worker. One cannot just run out of a conference room to avoid delivering a presentation.

When we most need our brain to engage we are left trying to play an advanced virtual reality game with hardware and programming built to play Pong.

FEAR IN THE DIGITAL AGE

To say we have not evolved when it comes to fear is not completely accurate. Contemporary writings and applied psychology today reference the 4Fs. Joining Flight or Fight are Freeze and Fawn. The latter two are typically linked to experiencing trauma and are being used to help those suffering from Post-Traumatic Stress and childhood trauma.

Freeze: A variation of the Flight response. Instead of fleeing a location you in essence flee in place. Because our physiological response to an attacking animal or a snarky comment from our boss is the same it would not be uncommon to react by not moving and remaining silent. Needless-to-say, freezing in a meeting has a different impact and/or meaning than it might in the presence of a threatening wild creature.

A variation on this theme is the concept of the cognitive effects of stress or fear. It is natural for one to experience the cognitive effects (i.e., brain burp, drawing a blank, etc.) when faced with a fearful situation.

Most of you have experienced this or seen it in action. Take the guy on Wheel of Fortune who can't get the letter everyone else knows. Even people who don't speak the language would get it. What's up with this guy?

Quite simply the lights, cameras, and knowledge that thousands are watching at home; would allow him to set a personal best in some physical endeavor, but his brain has taken a break. He is flush, heart is racing, and probably would take a bit of time to just remember his own name.

Fawn: Webster's Dictionary defines fawning as: 'trying to gain favor by acting servilely; cringe, and flatter.' When confronted by a fear stimulus one will try to put themselves in a better position by overtly complementing the person representing the threat. For example, a direct report receiving negative feedback, feeling at risk, and telling their boss what a wonderful leader they are. It should be noted that this is listed as a Co-Dependent personality type in trauma counseling.

Chapter 2

Fear and the Individual Contributor

"Every time you suppress some part of yourself or allow others to play you small, you are in essence ignoring the owner's manual your creator gave you and destroying your design."

Oprah Winfrey

Shortly after the Great Recession began, I started reflecting on fear and its impact on both individuals and organizations.

While working as a part-time adjunct professor I commuted to a satellite campus for my classes.

One evening I was walking toward my classroom and observed a supervisor berating his employee. They clearly were in the trades. Their tool belts being my first clue. I could not make out what was being said but the employee just stood there, head down, and took what the supervisor dished out. Abruptly the one-sided conversation ended and the supervisor walked to his truck and sped off. His employee, clearly shaken, just sat down on a nearby curb. His head in his hands.

I approached him and asked "Are you okay?"

He replied "No."

He said he was very upset and the worst was yet to come. His supervisor had asked if he had forgotten to bring the drill again. He started to respond that he left it in his bag in the truck. Unfortunately, instead of letting the young carpenter finish his supervisor launched his tirade.

"Why didn't you let your supervisor know before he drove off?" I asked

He stated "My boss was so angry I was afraid to say anything."

Uncomfortable with just letting the situation stand, I had my class start on an assignment so I could have a heart-to-heart with the supervisor when he returned. Felt it important to note that he had created a context for the miscommunication and that for his sake it might make sense to use a different communication style when things go awry in the future. Perhaps honor the fact that he had been designed with two ears and one mouth and that design might inform his ratio of time spent listening and speaking.

Over the years, many stories have surfaced where fear interferes with individual performance or success. This is one.

MASLOW REVISITED

It is not uncommon for a discussion about fear and the individual for Abraham Maslow's work to surface. Most have heard of Maslow's Hierarchy of Needs. Maslow had created a pyramid that ranged from Physiological Needs at its base and moving up through Safety, Love/Belonging, and Esteem Needs to the top tier of Self-Actualization.

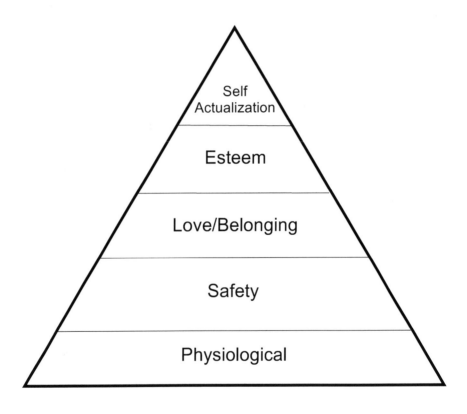

His work has relevance here for two reasons. First, you will note that the two categories that make up the foundation relate to physiological (known as basic needs) and safety needs. Both are major fear triggers.

So, when one's Physiological Needs (breathing, food, water, homeostasis) and Safety Needs (body, employment, resources, family, health, property) are threatened fear responses ensue.

Second, is the revelation his theory had been misconstrued for many years. In late1969 Maslow, a year prior to his passing, made what are referred to as The Maslow Tapes. In them he noted he had never intended the hierarchy be followed strictly in order. That is, in order to reach Self-Actualization, you must fulfill the needs below it on the pyramid. He noted different individuals will have different need levels. So, I might need to have my lower level needs only partially fulfilled to move toward Self-Actualization. He stated this is the only way one can explain the starving artists among us.

The ramifications for individuals at work, at home, and in their communities, are significant based on the two observations above. If one believes a bad decision at work might result in the loss of prestige, or position, or even their job; fear responses will be set in motion. If a change or action by another represents loss of health or property or employment or belonging the negative effects of fear will surely surface.

Additionally, when dealing with and motivating individuals we must consider their diverse levels of need up and down the pyramid. It will determine when and where one perceives a decision or action to be fearful. If someone has a need for high levels of Physiological and Safety Needs they are probably unnerved by mergers, layoffs, and changes in reporting relationships. All of which could impact their basic level needs.

If another person feels the basic needs are covered they may be more concerned by belongingness needs. At work, they will be more concerned about being in the know and attending all of the right meetings. Their friends, family, and coworkers are very important to them and any change in those relationships will set a fear response in motion.

One such individual is a surfer, Kaleo Roberson, from Maui, Hawaii.

Several years back, Kaleo was surfing a site known as Freight Trains (off Maalaea). Kaleo was in a group of 20 surfers waiting for the next wave. One of his eight-year old twin boys was in the group.

All of the sudden Kaleo noticed a shark circling his board.   He immediately went into Fight response punching the shark with his fist and then with his board.

According to a story in the Seattle Times, when asked if he was scared of the shark, Kaleo said "I don't care if this thing bites me, but if my pride and joys are making it to the beach safe, then I'll feed this thing my leg if I have to."

Clearly Safety Needs were subjugated to his Love/Belongingness Needs. The good news is that his boys are safe and sound and Kaleo has a memento of the occasion, a surfboard with a 14-inch shark bite taken out of it. As most parents know there are times when the safety needs take a back seat to protecting your family.

Continuing our discussion of needs, the individual who is concerned about Esteem Needs is going to be most concerned with those things that will put their status, respect for and of others, and self-esteem at risk. Fear stimuli will center around relationships marked by respect and trust. Anything that interferes or diminishes respect and self-esteem will produce a fear based response.

Finally, let's look at the Self-Actualized individual. This individual might appear to be unaffected by those things that prompt fear in others. Having the belief that the needs lower in the hierarchy are satiated their needs are more aspirational and nebulous. Their needs encompass things like morality, creativity, spontaneity, problem solving, lack of prejudice, and acceptance of fact.

The good news is that things like safety, love/belonging, and esteem are either met or irrelevant. At home, they feel needs are satiated and at work they are less concerned with layoffs, organizational changes, or reduction of benefits.

The bad news is that their sources of fear are less predictable and more difficult to anticipate and deal with. Their extremely high standards when it comes to morality, bias, and ethics might seem irrational to others, difficult to explain, and even more difficult to deal with once they perceive these values have been violated and are in jeopardy.

In the final analysis, Maslow's Hierarchy still has relevance when dealing with fear stimuli and response. It provides one way to look at fear and its wide-ranging impact on individuals both at work and in their personal lives.

Another lens for codifying fear and the individual is to look at specific types of fear. The remainder of this chapter is dedicated to the three most common individual fears; Fear of Making a Bad Decision, Fear of Loss, and Fear of Judgement.

FEAR OF MAKING A BAD DECISION

In thinking about this type of fear, a dear friend came to mind. He and his wife were looking to purchase a home in a Silicon Valley neighborhood approximately 25 years ago. At that time, the home was listed at $300,000 and they struggled with the decision. They began the process of checking with friends who already lived in the neighborhood as well as friends and co-workers. With each conversation, the correct decision became more complex.

Those living in the neighborhood provided the pluses: quiet neighborhood, friendly neighbors, and great schools enhancing the value of the homes.

On the other hand, there were friends who were trusted investment advisors. They too talked about the neighborhood and market, but referenced the original selling price in the mid-seventies, the inflated price relative to the original price, and the importance of making the right decision.

The final straw occurred when one friend stated "$300,000! That is a long way to fall." As a result, the potential buyers moved directly to a Freeze response, we are talking full blown analysis paralysis.

Unfortunately, once the decision process stalled another buyer surfaced, made an offer, and purchased the home. Homes in the neighborhood have never returned to the $300,000 price point. Even through the Great Recession prices continued to rise. There have been several demographic changes. Waves of immigrants, who wanted their children to go to the best schools, moved into the neighborhood over the years (Japanese, followed by Chinese, then Russian and German, and now Indian). Homes in the neighborhood now sell for $1,500,000.

It is not uncommon for individuals who are struggling with an important decision to Freeze or take Flight.

Where Fear Fails—Making a Bad Decision

You may know someone who:

- Lost a promotion because they feared what might happen if they made the decision to ask for it.

- Delayed or did not apply for a new job because they could lose their current job if someone found out. Typically, the search for a new job is motivated by reasonable job insecurity. Often times the end result is the loss of both the current job and the new job opportunity.

- Failed to make a purchase due to indecision only to find out the car, clothing, or piece of jewelry was no longer available when they finally decided to buy.

- Chose to remain silent because the decision to speak up was daunting only to learn the silence caused another harm or embarrassment.

- Failed to make a decision to avoid danger because someone might be offended by their action, resulting in injury to themselves or others.

- Feared the ramifications of deciding to enter into a life-long relationship only to see the love of their life move on and capture the heart of another.

- Delayed the introduction of an idea or enterprise only to see someone else leverage the idea.

- Failed to help someone in need because you just couldn't decide whether to intervene or not.

As you can see from these examples, an individual's fear of making a bad decision can have a significant and lasting impact.

FEAR OF LOSS

Living with my Grandmother (Nana) and Grandfather (Papa) during my freshman year of college, I found it curious that my Papa drove to his bank every morning. Nana would tease him about going to count his money.

"Hope it is all still there." She would say with a smile.

Papa would wave with dismissal and go off with a serious look on his face.

Later in life I learned Papa's fear of loss and miserly behaviors were more than reinforced by his history. Once a successful businessman in Honolulu he at one point lost everything. Family stories differ, but the ending is the same. He and his family moved to San Francisco and started over. This coupled with living through the depression led to guarded interaction with the world.

On one level his fear of loss served him well. As he aged he was less susceptible than his peers to the many frauds perpetrated against the elderly in our country. Papa made his trips to the bank, scrutinized his grocery receipts, and asked for the discarded parts from the car mechanic. He crafted a world where taking advantage of him would be difficult. And, I think this goes in the good column.

However, his circle of friends was limited and he found it difficult to trust most he came in contact with from the bank teller, to the grocery store clerk, to the car mechanic. His circle of trust was difficult to enter and remained small for the rest of his life. Unfortunate because he was smart, funny, and loved Nana more than life itself. If you were in his circle of trust, his spirit of Aloha and kindness were generous beyond belief. His fear of loss resulted in the loss of association with others.

Where Fear Fails—Loss

- The potential loss of a life partner keeps one from even pursuing a long-term relationship

- Fear of death prevents one from telling their doctor about a symptom that could uncover a life-threatening disease early enough to make a difference

- Not investing or saving because the markets might crash or banks could fail. The end result has the same destination, lack of savings for rainy days or a comfortable retirement

- The idea of losing a sale prevents a salesperson from asking the questions that would either improve their position or help them move on before investing too much time on a poor opportunity

- People so obsessed with the potential of losing their job getting fired due to poor performance

- Fear of losing a pet keeps people from the unconditional love a pet will bring. Not to mention the extended longevity contemporary studies now link to pet ownership

A theme that will surface again and again is how a fear often becomes a self-fulfilling prophecy. This theme is ever present in the examples above.

Fear of Loss becomes the very loss one fears.

FEAR OF JUDGEMENT

It has been said if you want to determine how important a topic is you just need to look at the number of movies made to address that topic. With the plethora of coming of age movies that have been made, sold, and watched there can be no doubt that the fear of being judged by others, sometimes labeled social anxiety, is one of the biggies. This concept has been reinforced by countless movies about awkward teens trying to fit in for as long as I can remember.

Here are a few that come to mind:

The Breakfast Club

Ferris Bueller's Day Off

Lean on Me

Dead Poet's Society

Mean Girls

Clueless

The Perks of Being a Wallflower

No doubt most of you can quickly create your own list. A Facebook post/thread in the making.

Fear of Judgement can lead to feelings of inadequacy, humiliation. embarrassment, and depression. The anxiety linked to these feelings is easy to relate to for many. Even the 'cool kids' in High School were confronted with being normal, and judged, at some point in life where their reputation was unknown and did not precede them. We gravitate to these movies because there always seems to be some sort of redemption. Our favorite flawed protagonists find out that others have similar experiences and in the end triumph.

However, in the real-world things have become a bit more complicated.

Snarky has not only become a word it has become fashionable. This coupled with social media and the ability to reach thousands makes it a very scary place for those who fear being judged and ridiculed by others. This is exacerbated by a feeling of anonymity when joining the fray online.

Social media has created a place where saying things we would not say in person, being cruel, and piling on is acceptable and commonplace.

A dear friend refuses to have a social media footprint. And, while she misses out on significant events regarding life-long friends, children, grandchildren, new pets, weddings, incredible vacations, and the passing of a friend. She also avoids being judged by people she has never met, hearing about someone's inane political views, or any of the other acts of silliness that occupy cyberspace.

While fear of judgement is common it should be noted not everyone has a concern about what others think of them. I'm sure someone in your life comes to mind. Narcissist and Ego-Maniacs aside, there are those who have healthy egos and the Fear of Judgement does not apply.

One way of looking at what might account for the diverse reactions to others' inputs is the concept of Locus of Control.

Internal and External Locus of Control

The premise of Locus of Control is an orientation or belief of whether your future is determined by your internal thoughts and actions or by external factors beyond your control.

Those with an Internal Locus of Control (sometimes referred to as Internals) believe their success going forward is determined by their thoughts and actions. They believe if something goes awry it is due to something they thought, said, or did; and can be repaired or recovered through their efforts. As one might guess, because they believe they are the masters of their destiny they are less apt to be concerned with what others think or say about them. Their focus is on what they must think, say, and do to create a positive future. Their positive focus tends to show in both their view of the world and their personality. It is not uncommon for Internals to leave behind acquaintances, co-workers, or organizations who choose to diminish them, or belittle them and their dreams. This tends to inoculate Internals from the Fear of Judgement.

External Locus of Control individuals (sometimes referred to as Externals) believe others, fate, chance, and the world around them determines success or failure. They believe bad things happen because of some force beyond their control. Because lack of control is a major stressor Externals tend to be unhappy with their circumstances and more pessimistic than their Internal counterparts. Because they believe change is beyond their control they often take no action unless it is supported or sanctioned by others.

It is not too far-fetched to think when you feel your actions, thoughts, and deeds do not make a difference you become more susceptible to outside forces and the opinions of others.

Self-Esteem

The link between Locus of Control and Self-Esteem is both intuitive and logical. If you believe life happens to you, that others' opinions of you determine who you are, and your success is guided by the actions, thoughts, and decisions of others; low self-esteem is a probable outcome.

It is important to note that both high and low levels of esteem can impact social acceptance. Arrogance or Low Self Opinion can result in the very judgement one seeks to avoid. In the case of low self-esteem, the door is wide open for the classic feelings associated with Fear of Judgement listed earlier in this section: inadequacy, humiliation. embarrassment, and depression.

The concern is that a self-fulfilling downward spiral takes hold. Feelings of inadequacy lead to non-participation or timid participation which drives judgement leading to humiliation or embarrassment, which in turn elicits a Flight or Freeze response. Which in turn makes one want to not participate and act strangely when they do.

Where Fear Fails—Judgement

The consequences of a Fear of Judgement; impacted by an external locus of control or poor self-esteem, can be dramatic:

- Failure to participate in social activities at school, work, or in a community for fear of being judged

- Withholding valuable contributions in meetings because others might challenge your ideas only to have someone else get credit and praise for what you were thinking

- Not sticking up for yourself or someone you care about because of what others might think. Giving the impression you are weak or not supportive.

- Not stepping up to an important presentation or speech because others might scrutinize the performance limiting your influence or ability to move up in an organization.

- Failure to publish that book you have always wanted to write because others might not find it interesting or worthwhile.

- Letting an entrepreneurial venture die before it gets started because it is possible no one will want to buy from or support the venture.

- Failing to pursue 'that thing' you have wanted to do since you were eight years old because others might criticize you. Sing on stage, act in a play, paint the world as you see it, or play in an orchestra or band.

INDIVIDUAL PLAYBOOK

Give Your Fears a Reality Check

Have you ever looked at someone in full fear mode and wondered why they were so worried, or afraid, or unable to see the situation clearly? Do you suppose others have viewed you in the same fashion?

Sometimes it is so clear from the outside of a challenge or problem and yet so daunting when you are in the middle of it.

Recently I joined my wife at a conference in Quebec City. While she attended the conference, I explored the beautiful city and its history. A primary goal for the week was to get out of the hotel room and get some much-needed exercise. So, off I went each morning.

On day two I decided I would climb the stairs to the Citadel perched above the Upper City. As I ascended the first flight of stairs I experienced a shortness of breath and minor vertigo. I reached the first platform and moved as far away from the railing that provided a wonderful view of the Lower City and river below. With my back against the back wall and people passing by I regained my balance and started up the second flight of steps. At this point I was passed by a group of Army Rangers sprinting up the steps and playing tag. During my ascent, I reflected on the fact that their movements and actions were much riskier than mine. It also hit me that from their perspective there is nothing risky about this trek at all.

As I arrived at the second plateau, I stood a bit closer to the rail and focused on my breathing. Then I saw it: a sign that referenced something pertaining to the Governor's Promenade or something of that ilk. And I immediately determined that no government would take the risk of being sued if someone fell from this path. I joined the children, parents, and Rangers now traveling back down. With the changed perspective I finished my climb, albeit still very cautious.

The reality check had served its purpose. For the remainder of the week I climbed to the Citadel each day without fear or caution. My wife walked with me on the final day. She said she was surprised the height was not bothering me. I just smiled.

Ask Good Questions

As with the situation above, sometimes it makes sense to take a deep breath and ask some really good questions to look at situation or challenge from a different perspective.

- What would Joe or Jill do?

- How might this look if it didn't involve me?

- What advice would I give a friend confronted with this fear?

Most motivational speakers from W. Clement Stone to Les Brown to Tony Robbins have spoken about a change in state or mindset (from fear to positive action) by asking the right questions. You see, our brains will provide answers to the questions we ask. If our brain doesn't know the answer, it will keep searching until it finds one.

So, if you ask fear-based questions:

- How will we possibly survive if I get laid off?

- How could I have been so stupid?

- What's the worst that can happen?

The answers your brain generates often will be negative and feed the fear.

However, if you ask positive questions:

- What is my exit strategy if I leave my current job?

- Given the situation I have created, how can I make it work out for the best?

- What's the best thing that can happen?

The answers to these questions will often ease the fear and lead to positive action.

Don't Rent Problems Before You Own Them

I have a circle of friends I admire a great deal. They are men and women who have accomplished a great deal in life and are people of the highest character. Needless-to-say, as we exchange stories about what has happened since our last visit, we sometimes share what concerns, difficulties, and fears we have.

It has become our inside joke to break up certain fear conversations with a simple statement: "Don't rent problems before you own them." You know the ones, they are the conversations that start out with 'What if....'"

We decided at some point in our time together, with plenty of data and case-based reasoning, that we spent a great deal of time worrying about what might happen. And, most of the time the next visit involved friendly teasing and laughing about how one of us had worried needlessly.

Two key points here:

- One way to reduce fear is to ask if we are being a bit pre-mature worrying about this problem, issue, challenge, or change.

- It is clear, while it may be prudent to challenge the 'rental agreement' unfortunately our programming lends itself to evaluating risk constantly. Give yourself a break when you rent and remember to ask good questions if you do.

Leveraging the Experience of Others

Modeling, that is finding someone who has done something well and emulate their behaviors, is often referenced in self-help and motivational literature. It is rare to discover a fearful situation that someone else hasn't already navigated. Although your worries may seem unique and one of kind more often than not someone has been there, done that, hated it, and got the tee shirt.

For example, it is estimated that of the 5.3 million people who experience social anxiety 74% of them fear public speaking.

Working with people who struggle giving presentations is one of my favorite coaching activities. The fear is significant and at times career limiting. The rewards and change in performance are always well worth the time and effort put into helping someone extinguish this fear.

Logic dictates that most audiences want you to do well. After all, who wants to sit through a boring or bad presentation? But, for those with this form of social anxiety the fear is palpable. And, once again our physiology betrays us. Dry mouth, weak knees, and brain freeze.

At a recent Effective Presentation work session, I took note of a particular participant who entered the room with his friends. He was talkative and outgoing. I watch for outgoing personalities in case I need to call on a volunteer to present first.

However, as soon as the session began and I outlined our day together he became very quiet and his whole demeanor changed. After modeling an effective presentation, and providing best practices I sought out volunteers to present and noted that he was doing his best to avoid eye contact. I decided to give him space hoping he would recover after seeing others present and receive feedback in a safe environment.

As we approached lunch, he was the last to go. He worked hard and his fear was visible. His peers smiled and nodded in agreement trying to urge him on. I am pretty sure he missed all of the non-verbal support they were providing. When his peers left for lunch he stayed behind.

He informed me that he would not be coming back from lunch. He just didn't think he would ever be able to present in front of a group. I felt badly for him and noted that he seemed very supportive of others while they were presenting. I told him I would be using the videos taken in the first round to provide feedback and suggestions prior to the second presentation. I asked if he would help me review each of the videos prior to departing for the day.

Over lunch we watched each short presentation and he noted what he liked and what he might instruct the presenter to do. I thanked him and he left for a late lunch.

Much to my surprise, he returned with the others and volunteered to go first in the second round. He courageously watched his first presentation with his peers and seemed to acknowledge how kind they were in providing feedback. He then stepped up and gave his presentation again.

The difference between the two presentations was so dramatic his peers gave him a standing ovation when he finished. Some even teased him about play acting the first time around. He brought his true, best self to the presentation.

He remained after the coaching session once again. He graciously thanked me for helping him break through. He informed me he felt extra pressure because his next promotion would require a great deal of presenting and he was extremely worried he would not be selected. With the juxtaposition of the two presentations I asked him what made the difference. He said he was so distracted when others were presenting that the morning was a blur. He said when he went through the videos he took the opportunity to see what worked and what didn't.

He noted "Everyone had good and bad parts to their presentation and with some minor teaks could be very good. And, by the way, no one died."

FYI: He got that promotion.

There is value in learning from others or looking at your fear from another perspective. Sometimes when you look at your fears through the eyes of another, your fears become more manageable. In the case of presentation coaching, the solution lies in providing a positive model of both presenting and coaching. In the case above he quickly engaged the model of 'to learn, teach.' Reviewing the videos and providing feedback was instrumental in his change.

Sometimes the difference between fear and courage is having a positive model to copy. When the path is charted for us we have a better chance of getting where we are going.

Fear at the individual level can be quite the challenge. As we have seen, our physiology is better suited for earlier times and different threats.

Additionally, fear linked to decisions, loss, or being judged by others can be paralyzing and often times can ensure the thing we fear most comes to fruition.

While these fears and our reactions to them might be unnerving there are personal strategies we can engage to mitigate our fears—doing a reality check, asking positively framed questions, and modeling the behaviors of those who have experience handling similar situations.

This examination of fear and the individual shows how complex fear and responses to it can be. Now imagine taking 10-12 unique individuals with unique personalities and fears and forming a cohesive, high-performing team. Let's look at fear, its impact on teams, and how to keep your team from becoming dysfunctional.

Chapter 3

Fear and the Dysfunctional Team

"When two men in business always agree, one of them is unnecessary."

William Wrigley Jr.

As a basic rule a team has one overarching goal, to achieve the results they were assembled to achieve. Whether a team of engineers, plumbers, athletes, salespeople, scientists, or healthcare professionals their goal is to achieve results that meet or exceed expectations.

Success or failure is determined by a number of factors. These factors often determine whether a team is high performing or dysfunctional.

Key among them are:

- Making timely decisions with the best information available

- Trusting relationships

- An environment where team members feel safe to contribute and bring their best self to the task at hand

- Communication and coordination contributing to team success

- A system of accountability

- Ability to navigate conflict in a positive way

- A Leader who knows the value and talents of each team member, removes barriers to success, and keeps the team on track

TEAMS, DECISION MAKING, AND GROUPTHINK

Over the past 30 years I have worked with teams of all types. They were short-term project or crisis oriented, long-term permanent, matrixed, large, small, co-located, and virtual. Each had its own personality and level of success.

One of the key factors impacting their success or failure was how decisions were made and implemented. In almost every case team cohesion, leadership approach, and how conflict was handled impacted the decision process. The most common scenarios where teams failed are captured in the descriptions below:

- The team leader made all important decisions without team input from those who needed to be on board to implement the decision resulting in poor execution.

- Team met several times a day for hours analyzing every aspect of the decision ad nauseam without ever coming to a resolution resulting in missed deadlines and loss of performance bonuses.

- Internal strife and unhealthy competition kept the team from reaching any form of consensus that would have moved the project forward and ensured success. Ultimately these teams were dispersed to other teams unfortunately in many cases taking their 'baggage' with them.

- Team dynamics created an environment where contribution and creativity were discouraged by the group leading to a lack of analysis and decisions made with bad or limited information.

Research into one area of study linked to the fear-based aspects of team decision making, labeled Groupthink, was introduced as early as the 1950's and resulted in the seminal work of Irvine Janis in the 1970's. Research continued through the 1990s and often sees a revival whenever team dynamics are discussed.

In its simplest form, Groupthink prevents critical evaluation and analysis in the pursuit of team harmony and coherence. Team members defer to the leader's decisions without question. Conflict and dissenting opinions are discouraged. Common examples are the Bay of Pigs, Pearl Harbor, the Baseball Umpires Strike, and Swissair.

Let's use events in Cuba as a lens for looking at Groupthink because it directly relates to a team and informs some of the fears discussed in the remainder of this chapter. Historical accounts note the differences between the failure of the Bay of Pigs Invasion and success in dealing with the Cuban Missile Crisis. Most accounts say the difference came down to President Kennedy's influence on decision making and team dynamics with regard to team member input.

In the case of the Bay of Pigs; President Kennedy lead every meeting, gave his opinion first before seeking input from the team, and key members of the team discouraged discourse. Consequently, true to its nature, Groupthink led to limited analysis and critique, and a disastrous outcome.

In contrast, during the decision process leading up to actions in the Cuban Missile Crisis President Kennedy chose to let others lead the meetings and in some instances, was absent from the meetings. Team member input and discussion was encouraged and supported. The byproduct was a well-thought out approach to dealing with the crisis.

Groupthink made its way into <u>Where Fear Fails</u> because it is enabled by three of the most common fears at the team level. So, it appeared to be a natural link for fear and dysfunctional teams.

As you might suspect, because a team is made up of individuals the fears discussed in Chapter 2 are ever-present. In fact, looking at the three fears in this chapter you might see some natural affinities. For example, Fear of Judgement and Fear of Public Embarrassment. Let's take a closer look.

FEAR OF PUBLIC EMBARRASSMENT

While working with a proposal team an interesting example of the fear of public embarrassment surfaced. The team had worked hard for months on a particular sales opportunity. The opportunity was considered very important and the client would be great for the company's growth and reputation. The team had put together a proposal, had provided written responses to questions about the proposal, and navigated the competition from six contenders to the final two. The presentation was the culmination of all of their hard work. The thought of losing this late in the process was viewed through the lens of the time, effort, and resources that went into winning this opportunity.

My client had assembled a 'red team' of technical experts, executives, and myself serving as a presentation coach. We dedicated a full day to evaluate the sales presentation, with breaks to do other work that needed to be done by the team members. The morning moved forward with minimal interruptions. I became a bit concerned that there were very few interruptions or critiques.

During the first break two technical experts came up to me with their thoughts. Both had suggestions on how the presentation could flow better. One expert said the presentation was designed in a way that it hid one of the company's strongest assets. It seemed odd they did not provide feedback real time so the presentation team could tweak the presentation in the moment.

When we reconvened, I asked about the suggestions and checked for acceptance. I offered the two engineers an opportunity to clarify my statements to ensure accuracy. Both declined. The red team discussed the inputs, added their thoughts, and the presentation team was asked to present that portion of the presentation again with the new approach. It worked well.

Despite the most senior executive encouraging inputs real time, the next two hours played out in the same fashion. The team presented without feedback and we moved toward the next break. Again, more red team members approached with inputs. And, again, we used the inputs to improve the presentation when the team reconvened.

When the day concluded, I spoke with a few of the executives. I asked if there was some protocol or unspoken rule about interrupting the presentation. They said no, that the red team actually works better when feedback is provided real time.

I also spoke with one of the technical experts. He said he would love to provide the feedback in the moment, but is concerned about being wrong and embarrassing himself in front of the executives.

The good news is the team incorporated the inputs in fine fashion and won the business.

My concern, what happens if there isn't an outsider present willing to serve as a conduit for inputs from those who fear embarrassment.

Where Fear Fails—Public Embarrassment

The fear of public embarrassment often results in the suppression of information or concerns that could alter an outcome. Here are a few examples:

- A leader responds negatively to an employee's input during a team meeting and is surprised when his team no longer contributes during meetings.

- Team member hesitates to share concern about an upcoming deliverable for fear of making a fool of themselves, resulting in a missed deadline.

- Failure to bring attention to a quality issue because of the potential of being wrong leading to shipping a flawed product or having to do rework to get the product up to code.

- Not providing solid, constructive feedback in a peer review for fear of retaliation and embarrassment.

- Not being fully engaged because a prior act earned both teasing and a nickname from the team.

FEAR OF CONFLICT

Early in my career I worked for a small corporate training team that supported a very large corporation. We covered all leadership, negotiating, effective presentations, and ethics training for a company of 35,000. Needless-to-say we ran lean and depended on every team member to do their part. We were a diverse group and had both early career and former retirees on staff.

As we were approaching overload our leader worked on an additional headcount. The team was beyond ecstatic to hear we would have an additional team mate. The interviewing process began and three viable candidates surfaced. We decided to do team interviews to determine the top candidate.

One in particular looked great on paper and interviewed well. He was well-spoken, had a Master's degree from a top school, and seemed comfortable in front of the team. The only warning sign, an occasional defensive response when discussing the challenges of the position. We decided to move forward with this candidate without any discussion about team dynamics or chemistry.

Shortly after his orientation day things began to break down. While discussing team assignments and where he might add value in the classroom he informed the team that he had a process for getting ready to train and would need some time. The next day he arrived well after the rest of the team, secluded himself in a conference room and started prepping.

Historically, a new team member would be assigned a course to be co-trained with an experienced trainer. The team expressed concern that he was not engaging his co-trainers in his prep.

A week passed with no contact, no request for assistance from the senior co-trainers, or questions about how the training was designed. He arrived late for team meetings. Any planning discussion that involved courses he was scheduled to deliver brought argument, resistance, and what appeared to be angry expressions. It should be noted that no one escaped his wrath, from the most assertive among us to our wonderful conflict avoiders, everyone got a turn in the hot seat.

His private prep sessions now included putting chart paper over the glass door so no one could 'spy' on him and a locked door. The fight and flight responses probably have not escaped you at this point. Six months passed without him delivering a course. The team rallied around the flag and covered his absence. After all the show must go.

Attempts to engage ended. The team shifted scheduling to a separate team meeting which he chose to skip. No mention of his behaviors took place as a team, from team leaders, or individually. It became clear the team had chosen harmony over confronting non-performance. Conflict avoidance was ever-present, overt, and placed a great deal of pressure on a team already stretched beyond reason.

Finally, when top performers started looking for other positions within the corporation our leaders stepped up and came to a mutual agreement that the situation was not working for all concerned. He left without entering the classroom to observe or train, having received a salary the entire time. Rumor was that he also received a severance package.

Fear of conflict both at the peer and leader level created a context for poor performance and focus on an individual team member instead of the team's mission. As is typically the case, fear of conflict extracted a great cost. Within a year almost the entire staff had returned to retirement or found work elsewhere in the corporation.

Where Fear Fails—Conflict

A team is often impacted when healthy dialogue and dissent is squelched. Decisions fall prey to Groupthink or are made with limited information

- A leader creates an environment where any divergent opinion is considered conflict and barred. This creates a context where well-informed contrarian views are stifled to the detriment of team results.

- Team avoids conflict at all cost, leading to festering ill will and hallway conversations all leading to a lack of trust and team dysfunction.

- The team leader responds to reasonable feedback with anger and personal attack. A fawn response is typical, shutting down all future feedback and leaving the leader with the misguided impression they are doing a good job and all is well with their team.

- Healthy conflict and debate give way to passive-aggressive behaviors and snarky comments. Again, trust and team performance are the casualties.

- Team leader fails to provide important feedback or report team challenges to avoid conflict with their boss. The team sees this as weakness and a lack of support. Ultimately if a leader is not willing to stand up for their team, team loyalty wanes.

- An aggressive, combative customer is placated to avoid conflict. In most cases the customer gets what they want, shows no loyalty, and writes a negative Yelp review. Team cohesion suffers.

FEAR OF BEING AN OUTLIER

Okay, full disclosure here, I am one of those people who watches those silly reality shows. Something about seeing how people behave when stressed is just fascinating to me. While they state: "This is just a game, I am different at home." What I see is how a person acts when under stress and in pursuit of wealth.

One observation I have formed over the years is that the most stressful times occur when someone is alienated from the 'power alliance.' Once it is evident that conversations are taking place without them, the outlier normally reacts in one of two ways.

In one scenario, the person at risk fights to stay on the island or in the house. They try to move attention to someone else who deserves eviction more. Or they try to make the case for keeping them around. They are clearly in Fight response. Their aggressive or passive aggressive behaviors normally become the case for their eviction.

In contrast, some others choose to lay low or hide. They go off by themselves and guarantee they are no longer present for important conversations or strategy sessions. When they do surface, all conversations stop until they depart. Increasing their paranoia. This Flight response typically results in further alienation and eventually eviction.

The typical team environment is not much different from the island or a house where you are stuck with your housemates with cameras filming 24/7. If a team member feels different from everyone else, not included in key discussions or decisions, not as smart as others, or not valued; they will also exhibit one or more of the 4F fear responses. The stress of goal achievement coupled with alienation is a recipe for disaster.

Where Fear Fails—Being an Outlier

Being ostracized by a team or group prompts strong fear responses that almost always lead to team dysfunction. Here are a few examples:

- A team member who feels alienated becomes disruptive, inserting themselves into discussions and interrupting others mid-sentence. In response, other team members seek to have discussions over lunch, in the parking lot, or after work; further isolating their peer.

- The leader of a team unconsciously makes certain team members feel like outsiders actively displaying an affinity for team members who remind her of herself. Choice assignments and high visibility opportunities were all funneled to her 'favorites.' As a consequence, despite needing everyone to produce the outliers began to struggle and underperform.

- A long-standing, close knit team experienced a leadership change. Without awareness or cause, the team limited its information sharing, questions, and support. The new leader, feeling alienated and at risk, demanded respect and inclusion. This did not play well and the team withdrew further.

- Having received several awards for top performance a team member also received an onslaught of reproach from her peers. The critiques almost always related to being political with higher ups, totally ignoring the real reasons she received the accolades. The end result was a diminishing of the top performers' contributions and overall team performance.

- A young engineer worked on a project which he tried to socialize with his team and his manager. The team and its leader were single focused, totally consumed with the work at hand and consequently ignored him and his project. Imagine their surprise when the young alienated engineer struck out on his own and started one of the most profitable businesses in Silicon Valley.

TEAM LEADER PLAYBOOK

This chapter began with a discussion about the overarching purpose for a team, achieving results. We explored three of the fears that get in the way of that purpose. Here are a few recommendations on how team leaders can mitigate those fears.

Communicate Early and Often

One of the best ways to inoculate your team from fears that impede their success and progress is to communicate what you can early and often.

Acknowledging limits placed on team leaders by their bosses and organizations to hold information close to the vest. You should seek to share what you can. Your information will always be more accurate and informed than what your team creates on their own.

I once worked with a Physician who railed against sites like WebMD. Her concern was her patients' imagination when informed by limited data. She said that someone with acne can go on WebMD and convince themselves they have leprosy. Your team will be equally creative if left to their own devices.

While you may not be able to talk about the final implications of a change, you can discuss a likelihood that a change will occur, and you will provide details as soon as they are finalized. As soon as possible, communicate why a change is happening and what it means to them (the team). The focus should be on them and their interest first. Beyond the "Why This, Why Now" if you don't speak to their issues first they will not hear one word until you do.

A note here, many organizations delay communications because they are afraid there will be a talent drain if they do. In fact, if there is a great deal of uncertainty the fears described in this chapter will surface and your best and brightest will be looking for new opportunities.

Be Empathetic

When team members or your team as a whole begin to display some of the symptoms of fear be available (physically and mentally) and create a safe place where they can share.

Bottom Line: Lead with listening not lecturing.

After acknowledging the reactions to fear, use simple questions to get at the source:

"Sounds like you are feeling at risk, tell me what's going on?"

"I've noticed that we have missed a couple deadlines and we work hard as a team to meet all deliverables, what are your thoughts?"

"We strive to have zero defects, and have been slipping a bit lately. I'm open to your thoughts."

The questions above are not 'the questions' or something for you to memorize and repeat. Instead they represent a pattern. State what is expected and observed, then open the door for them to share. It doesn't matter what words you use as long as the end result is you listening to what is creating a challenge for them and the source of their fears. Once you have unearthed what is bothering them, fully understand their perspective, then you can begin to work on resolution. Please note there is no attempt to justify their actions or read their minds by asking 'Is it because _____?"

The goal here is empathy, understanding their perspective and hearing their thoughts. It is not about showing how smart you are or sharing stories about how you handled things in the past.

Meet Them Where They Are

Once you understand team member concerns from their perspective you can provide support and counsel. The key here is to not rush the process. It is natural, once you understand, to leverage your years of experience and go into solve mode.

Unfortunately, if you encourage others to hurry up, start the car, and drive off before everyone is in the vehicle the process will actually take longer than a more measured approach. This 'short cut' almost always ends up with you doing a U-Turn, picking up and buckling in those left behind, and retracing your path.

By attacking an issue from their starting point instead of your own you are available to travel along-side and see things from their perspective. This approach limits taking on the problem as your own or recommending a solution that only makes sense to you.

It also keeps autobiographical references in check. It is not uncommon for us to want to share our history and what we did when confronted with a similar experience. The problem is that the story/information may not resonate or make sense to them. It is the opposite of meeting them where they are. How many times have you had someone share an experience leaving you asking "What does that have to do with me?"

If you make the effort to truly understand where they are, what they are feeling, and the thoughts they have about resolution; you have a much better chance of moving things along and coming up with a solution that will be implemented and sticks.

Be Available

Needless-to-say, you have a much better chance of observing fear at the team level if you are present to do so.

This is not about telling the team that you have an open door. It is about being on the floor, in the virtual conference room, or popping into the cubicles. Again, it is about being present physically and mentally. It is difficult to have your finger on the pulse of your team if you are never with the team except for team meetings on some planned schedule.

If you take opportunities to be present then it becomes part of how things are done. When the Apple Watch says it's time to stand, why not take a stroll through the team area. When lunch or other needs call add to your daily steps where the team is working. If a team member wants to chat take a walk so that neither of you are tempted by phones, email, or text.

By making this standard practice there is less chance the work stops when the 'boss' arrives. It also increases the likelihood that your team members will leverage the opportunity to share issues, concerns, and challenges.

Whether you call it Management by Walking Around or some other coined phrase, the purpose is the same. Be present when and if something is getting in the way of your team achieving their results.

Now that we have had an opportunity to look at individual and team fears, let's expand the view further and look at how fear can place your organization as a whole at risk.

Chapter 4

Fear and the Organization at Risk

"Change before you have to."

Jack Welch

"May you live in interesting times!" Several years ago, while working as an Organizational Effectiveness (OE) consultant, this blessing (or curse) came to fruition.

The large company I worked for had just approved a merger and our location was rumored to be going from 35,500 employees to somewhere around 7,000. Speculation was Headquarters for the corporation would move and redundant roles (read people) would be eliminated. It was more than likely employees would be offered a chance to move or accept an exit package.

To put this in perspective, we are talking the equivalent of a small town disappearing. Our corporate campus had a Department of Motor Vehicles office, a Credit Union and Bank, our own fire department, a dry cleaner, and several restaurants and delis.

The time between the initial announcement and the merger becoming official passed very quickly. In the interim the OE staff put things in place to prep executives and mid-level leaders to discuss the change with the organization. We built 90-minute work sessions for all managers on organizational change and the fear responses we anticipated. We also worked with our Human Resource counterparts to get an idea of how big the change was going to be and what needed to be communicated and when.

When the day arrived to implement the change, we initiated our plan. The executives did their best to communicate Why we merged, why we did it at this point in our history, and what it meant to the employees. They were peppered with questions and the fear responses were unmistakable.

In the months that ensued we dealt with the ramification of the change. There was a spike in both sexism and race complaints, reduced sharing and communication from those trying to ensure they were the only one with specific pieces of key information (job security measure), and an increase in conflict and angry interactions. Because of the conflict and anger we added 'workplace violence awareness' to the manager's training two weeks prior to a potential shooting incident in a training trailer. It may have saved some lives that day.

As each wave of layoffs took place things became more intense and stressful. For the survivors; loss of life-long friends (peers and managers), thoughts of being unemployed, and workplace conflict took its toll on them personally and professionally. Worries about losing one's job resulted in missed goals and deadlines that ensured the very outcome the survivors were trying to avoid.

When it was announced that the merger had been successful and there would be no more downsizing the new organization went to work. Well, kind of. Actually, our work had just begun. The new teams exhibited what we labeled 'heritage bias.' Managers favored the employees from their prior company regardless of skill level. In meetings when employees and managers introduced themselves they used their prior company name instead of the new corporate name or work unit. 'That's not how we did it at Company X," became a common refrain.

We created and instituted a strategy for the next phase. Executives laid out their expectations for moving forward in the new organization. New badges were issued for everyone, removing any semblance of the 'good old company.' We also created and delivered more manager training addressing expectations for managers and how they might deal with employee concerns and resistance to change.

This scenario has played out in countless organizations with predictable results if not handled well. Over the past 15 years, 43% of all merged firms worldwide reported lower profits than comparable non-merged firms (Gugler, et al., 2003) and a recent KPMG study indicated that 83% of merger deals failed to boost shareholder returns.

Clearly this issue and others impacting both public and private organizations warrant attention and focus at all levels of leadership. Let's do a deeper dive by looking at Fear of Attack, Fear of Extinction, and Fear of Loss.

Fear of Attack

There is a concept in organizational psychology known as 'Equifinality.' It states that there are many paths or means to a single outcome. When it comes to organizational attacks the concept is spot on.

Organizations in today's hypercompetitive environment face a multi-faceted attack from multiple sources. They range from theft of intellectual capital to sensitive information being captured and held for ransom, from disclosure of secrets by employees to cyberattacks. Threats to organizations can come from the outside from competitors, black hatters, or regulators. They can also be internal in nature through employee error, apathy, or defection.

While concern about any and all of these threats is reasonable, responsible, and healthy; organizations who let fear interfere with the good conduct of their business or organizational mission pay dearly for their obsession.

When fear of attack becomes all consuming, organizations and the people who run and work for them exhibit behaviors that are abhorrent under normal conditions.

A case in point, we have a wonderful couple living next door to us. They are in their late eighties and are the kindest people you could ever meet. He holds several patents for a major automaker, and loves to tinker around the house and yard. She is a retired nurse full of care and compassion. Over the years, family visits to the Central Valley always concluded with her at our door with a bag full of fresh fruit or vegetables.

This beautiful couple met in the Japanese relocation camps in California's Central Valley. They are two of the most patriotic individuals I have ever met and yet the U.S. Government, with the implied consent of its citizens, and fearing attack confined them and took everything their families owned.   And, they have never once complained. They would have never even discussed this terrible time in our history had we not asked where they met and how long they have been married.

The fear of attack can extract a dear price if left unchecked and unquestioned.

Where Fear Fails—Attack

Below are some examples of the cost of unbridled fear of attack:

- A small corporation became concerned about corporate espionage and moved to inoculate themselves from outside access to their intellectual capital. They ran a lean operation with just enough employees to sell to and serve their clients. The arduous new security procedures and 'defense' mechanisms so impacted their operations that clients began switching to their competitors.

- A highly-regarded Healthcare organization became very concerned about moving to Electronic Health Records (EHR) shortly after the Affordable Care Act became law. Their prime concern was for the protection of patient information when medical records were transferred from paper to electronic format. How would they protect it within HIPAA guidelines? Unfortunately, their fears and consequent delay in implementation put them outside of the deadlines to receive Center for Medicare and Medicaid Services incentives. Money that could have assisted with the cost of implementation instead of creating an unfunded budget item.

- A major software/hardware developer created a new operating system and computers running that operating system. They made this move to prevent a competitor from chipping away at their market share. Instead of creating an alliance with others in the industry, they made the decision to bet on the new operating system and sell computers exclusively designed to use it. After an initial surge and grace period, sales began to decline. The new operating system resulted in limited software for a myriad of purposes, and made it difficult to migrate current computers to the new system. Eventually the company was acquired by a competitor who keep the part of the business it needed to fill a void, and discarded the rest along with the remaining employees.

Fear of Extinction

Fear of Extinction may be the one organizational fear most prone to Self-Fulfilling Prophecy. The language involved with this fear tends to underscore an impending disaster for the organization. Unfortunately, the disaster, instead of what needs to change, tends to become the focus of the organization.

We have alluded to the concept of Self-Fulfilling Prophecy a couple of times in earlier chapters. Self-fulfilling Prophecy states that a prophecy or belief comes to fruition through language dictating actions. If we state a day will be 'good' or 'bad' our conscious and unconscious mind drives actions making the outcome come true.

I have worked with or for several organizations who feared a change that might render them obsolete, optional, or bankrupt. They used several phases, all variations on the same theme, to describe the current situation:

"We are in dire straits."

"We have not had a good year in years placing us a risk."

"The business is not producing. We can't keep this up much longer."

"We need to chart a new course the old way just won't work anymore."

"Burn the boats this is our new world. We have no option."

Organizations then took actions based on and informed by these proclamations. Business units and structures changed and reorganized. Pricing models and approaches were modified. Marketing materials and logos were altered. New roles were created to address the new business models or approach to the marketplace.

Some organizations consolidated decentralized functions. Others regionalized formerly centralized functions. The changes came quickly often without input from those most impacted by the changes.

Long flights and plenty of time to reflect lead to long emails from CEOs. Executive retreats with high visibility and low information sharing created strategies and policies to support transformations. Committees with no formal charter were formed to address business crises. All the while, the rumor mills were active and in most cases spread rumors that were much worse than reality.

In many cases, the end result was a continued decline of the business, reduced market share, and mergers to remain a going concern.

Wear Fear Fails—Extinction

The fear of extinction often creates a context for organizational failure.

- Mid-sized, highly respected business services company showed stagnant growth and decided to change their go to market strategy, marketing, and offering. The changes resulted in a minimal increase in new clients and the loss of many former clients who no longer recognized the firm they had worked with for years. The company had solid business operations and cash on hand. Consequently, they were acquired by a competitor. The intellectual capital was reinstated to its original form and added to the new company's portfolio. Most of the former employees were terminated.

- International organization struggling to remain a going concern decided to move to an agency model and layoff its fulltime salesforce to reduce the cost of sales. The agency fees increased the bottom line initially but did not represent recurring funds. Negotiating with disparate entities, selling to the agencies at reduced prices, and lack of familiarity with products and valued customers put the company at the brink of bankruptcy. An investor group acquired the company at a discount.

- Following the downturn in 2008-2009 a mid-sized company decided to reduce their US footprint and actively expand into international markets. While this strategy made sense in the moment it has failed to produce the long-term benefits. The US market has improved and the void filled by a competitor. Exchange rates, diverse customs policies, and shipping costs have made the situation almost untenable.

In each of these examples smart people made reasonable decisions based on extinction being the most likely outcome if nothing changed. Thoughts of going out of business created thoughts and actions ensuring that result. What if these and other companies had asked different questions focused on success as a going concern instead of extinction? Would the decisions and consequences have been altered?

Fear of Loss

While there are some similarities to the fear of loss at the individual level, loss at the organizational level is often more complex and its impact more extensive. Like individuals, organizations are diverse. Some are publically held corporations with a fiduciary relationship with stockholders, some are public entities tied to local, state, or federal governments responsible to residents and taxpayers. And some are private corporations whose key fiduciary relationship is to their customers or clients.

During a recent discussion with a friend I asked about her thoughts regarding the greatest fear for corporations in today's environment. She has a background in finance and makes staying informed regarding finance and economics a priority. So, I value her perspective and opinion.

Her response: Publically held corporations most fear loss of value, in particular stock market valuation.

Influenced by shareholder inputs, demands, and pressures; decisions about where to spend capital, who should be on the executive team, and what to say in public forums, are viewed through the lens of how it impacts value. When things are going well corporations flourish and stock prices normally respond. Typically, this results in executives and board members having long tenures and little discussion about their actions or pay.

However, when things start heading in the wrong direction fear of loss encompasses loss of support, loss of stock value, and loss of shareholder support. Executive actions and compensation come under scrutiny. The board and executives become ever vigilant about what business journals and business networks are saying. Emotions and fear surfaces and informs actions. The problem is, as most stock analyst and executives will tell you, business decisions are best served by facts not emotions.

Fear stokes shifts in strategy, leadership changes, and terminations. Thoughtful and measured approaches to a disruption are replaced with responses to even minor status changes, often leading to decisions made with single data points.

While loss of value most likely holds the top spot for public corporations there are other forms of loss that impact them, public organizations, and private corporations. For example, loss of culture or fear of losing key customers and employees.

As noted in the introduction to this chapter, mergers and acquisitions do not have the best track record over the past 15 years. One key component here is the loss of organizational culture. The very culture that created organizational success in the first place.

Cultures actually define who organizations are and how they interact with customers, clients, the public at large, and employees. A culture change can impact business or public support. When successful organizational cultures give way to a new, blended, or modified form; government entities who once enjoyed service awards, can lose favor and acquire poor reputations despite the dedicated professionals who show up for work on time every day.

A business might decline due to resistance to change from employees and customers. More often than not those supporting the change in culture fail to seek the counsel of those most impacted by the change. The fear of loss hits those clients and employees and some common fear responses are typical: resistance, questioning, and in some cases termination of the relationship. The latter describes the third and final loss in this section, the loss of a key customer or employee.

When revenues decline due to clients leaving, the fear of loss can generate some unique behaviors further alienating clients/customers. For example, a Fight response might result in criticizing those who have left inappropriately in front of other clients. First, your customers talk either in person or online in sites like Yelp! Second, you have just left the client you were speaking with questioning what you say behind their back. A Fawn response might lead to 'begging' clients to return at a reduced price or with some other incentive. Desperation may not be the best marketing tool to entice former customers to return.

Needless-to-say, loss of an employee follows a similar script. Fear responses to the loss of key employee typically fall in the Fight or Fawn categories and get the attention of other employees you would like to keep on payroll.

Where Fear Fails—Loss: Value and Culture

Fear of Loss at the organization level can have far-reaching impact on organizations, their leaders, their employees, and those they serve.

- In response to a shrinking market share the founders of a mid-sized company looked for an investor to purchase their business. Fear of lost value resulted in an investment group with no experience in their industry purchasing the company at a discount. The new owners shifted the business model from a sales-driven culture to an order-taking culture. They increased warehouse and administrative personnel and decreased the sales force. Just prior to the going under the remaining salespeople put a deal together to buy the company and return the company to its former glory.

- Following a major reorganization combining departments a County Agency experienced a major shift in cultures. With the new, diluted culture employees became confused, distracted, and in some cases totally disengaged. This led to longer response times, citizen complaints, mission creep, and loss of key employees who transferred or retired.

- Negative press coverage led the Board of Directors of a large regional company to fire one of its founders. Employees and customers alike saw this individual as the face and voice of the company. Fear of a major change in culture and approach to business drove away loyal customers and set in motion the exodus of top employees loyal to the founder. Loss of market share and decreasing stock valuation have plagued the company ever since.

- A form of loss of value plays out in tens of thousands of public and private organizations each year. Fearing loss of standing and budget entities go on a spending spree in the final months of their fiscal year. The goal is to spend every penny of their budget so it will not be reduced next year. At a time when lean operations are all the rage, organizations are spending needlessly on items that end up in a closet.

Executive Playbook

The difference between organizational success and failure often turns on what is communicated, how it is communicated, who is included, and thoughtful decisions sans emotion. Here are a few thoughts on how executives can help their organizations navigate change, reduce fear, and create a context for success.

Communicate, Communicate, Communicate

Fear of the unknown is a natural byproduct of our judging nature. Uncertainty's impact on an organization's productivity and success is visible and real. However, concerns over lost productivity or loss of key employees can lead executives to hold information about an impeding change close to the vest.

The reality is that the rumor mill is already interrupting good conduct of your operations. Your key employees, hearing the rumors, are already tuning up their resumes.

To avoid a Pollyanna moniker, let me state I understand there are times when it is not appropriate to disseminate information and there are certain types of information that require great care.

That said, to successfully implement an organizational change typically requires communicating early and often. Any change that will require the support or actions of your workforce requires that you socialize that change well before it takes place. Resistance, anger, subterfuge, and palace uprisings can be mitigated by providing information to those who are most impacted by the change. Communication should launch the change and continue during the transition to the new situation. Once the change has been implemented, executive communication should provide updates on the outcomes expected from the change and any course corrections being made.

While discretion and thoughtfulness should guide your release of information, successful change typically favors those who communicate early and often. Employees should never be surprised by feedback about performance or their status in the organization.

Seek Input from Those Most Affected

C-Level executives and their public government counterparts often take the full burden of their organization on their shoulders. Believing they alone must figure out how to propel, motivate, and problem-solve.

Heroics aside, revisiting equifinality may be in order. If there are many paths to an outcome doesn't it make sense to involve others in creating a strategy. It may be that the solution to successfully navigate a major change is an amalgam of approaches. One source of data to inform your decision should be those most affected by the decision. When decisions are made with stakeholder inputs they tend to be better.

One of the methods you can employ is the 'skip-level' meeting. This is a way to get feedback and inputs from one or two levels down in the organization without filtering from your direct reports. Of paramount importance, you must create a safe environment to receive feedback. Inputs from these meetings should be used to inform the decision and not for punitive actions against the managers excluded from these meetings.

Demonstrating your commitment to anonymity may take a few sessions to accomplish. Once you have received and properly used the feedback provided once or twice, the rumor mill will take care of any concerns. The time will be well spent. The best decisions are enlightened by the thoughts and concerns of the employees and consumers most affected by the change.

Another approach to change strategy is to hold stakeholder meetings with clients, customers, or constituents. These meetings should focus on where you are exceeding expectations. It should also seek feedback on things you could do better and things you do well that have no perceived value to those who use your services or products. The latter could provide some cost savings if no longer provided.

Avoid Making Decisions Based on Emotions

As you probably gleaned, most of the examples in this chapter have a common theme. Fear drove emotions that guided decisions and actions. Here's the challenge, when emotion is grounded in fear the brain is not always fully engaged.

Your managers, employees, and external stakeholders will often react to a change with emotions. Fear may manifest as anger, silence, pouting, depression, resistance, malicious obedience, or surrender. While natural responses they do not create an environment well suited for making sound, well-informed decisions.

You, as executives or senior administrators, are held in high regard and at times appear to be immune to fear and emotions. However, when your decisions impact your organization, your employees and their families, and potentially the communities you live in, it is understandable that emotions will surface. The burdens you take on no doubt weigh heavy on you and lead to some sleepless nights.

The good news is that you are in your current role because you displayed the talents and skills to lead others and deal with challenges. When stress and fear emerges, relying on your experience and skills to mitigate it makes a great deal of sense. In order to leverage your skillset, you must first create some space between your fear response and the decision-making process. In essence we need to get the vessels that supply blood to our brains to dilate. This normally requires focusing on a different situation, thought, or even location. Once you take the energy out of the situation then you can use your ability to collect and analyze information to mitigate the fear. You will quickly begin to ask questions aimed at putting the challenge into perspective, formulating strategy, and determining who else should be involved in the solution.

Inviting others into the problem-solving process is another means for reducing the fear response and help you hone your decision and approach. Sharing accountability for the solution will naturally counter some of your physiological responses to the fear.

We have now reviewed fear, physiological responses, and how humans react. Additionally, we have looked at the debilitating effects of fear on individuals, teams, and organizations. After 30 years of working with individuals, leaders, and organizations it is my observation that most fear stimulus in organizations occurs naturally without a leader's intent to use fear as a tool or leadership approach. However, there have been occasions to observe first hand those who do.

Where Fear Fails would be incomplete without a discussion of fear as an intentional leadership philosophy and methodology.

Chapter 5

Fear as a Leadership Approach

"People don't resist change. They resist being changed!"

Peter Senge

We sat across from each other at lunch. The conversation moved from how the team was struggling to a focus on my numbers. My situation, having been set up for success in his view, perplexed my boss. After all, the others had relevant challenges in their territories. According to my boss, I had plenty of untapped opportunities and no real excuses.

It appeared the messages were delivered with a certain zeal from my perspective. When the review was complete he asked for my thoughts. I spoke to challenges my clients were facing and how they were not only using dollars but time normally be earmarked for us. This was met with an animated response that none of my peers where seeing that in their territories.

He expressed that the situation could not continue and asked what I was going to do to change it. I was silent. Freeze response in action. It was building well before the question. Flush, heart racing, dry mouth, and narrowed focus on his expression. On some level the near smile seemed incongruent with the conversation. He said he would give me a few minutes to think about it and went off to the restroom.

The break gave me a chance to regroup both physically and mentally. I quickly formulated a strategy and wrote it down. Upon his return, I presented my thoughts and how I might improve my numbers. He said he hoped it would be enough and that he expected my best efforts.

Shortly after dropping him off at the airport I began calling my peers and expressed by concern about being fired. To a person, they laughed and shared their version of 'the talk.' Contrary to what I was told, they had all shared a concern about client budgets and distractions with our boss. For those leaders who choose to use fear as a motivator, please know your employees do talk. Playing loose with the facts will not serve you well.

This scenario played out several times over the years. Some years we were the team to beat or at least had individual performers lauded by the company. Other years we performed well below our capabilities. The best I can tell, there was no direct correlation between fear as a leadership tool and our success.

Let's look at a few of the reasons why fear often fails as an intentional leadership approach.

Efficacy

One of the major reasons fear fails as a leadership approach is our response to the stimuli as outlined throughout this book.

If our goal is to get a person's attention, motivate them to perform, and have them bring their best self to the task at hand; our coded responses to fear are probably not optimal.

For Example:

- Goading an employee into a loud and public argument and expecting them to quickly regain composure and get back to the task at hand.

- What is the benefit of having a direct report hide in the supply room, lunch room, or restroom after a particularly embarrassing public scolding.

- It is difficult to fathom how challenging an employee during an important presentation would enhance their delivery.

- Having a direct report focus on praising your leadership style instead of focusing on the feedback, albeit harsh, that you just provided.

It is clear fear inducing threats, arguments, scolding, or public embarrassments are more apt to inhibit than motivate. Fear as a leadership tool impedes progress, detracts from healthy team dynamics, and builds resentment.

Ultimately the leader's behavior becomes the focus instead of enhanced performance and improved results.

Shelf Life

To say that fear, as a leadership device, always fails would be inaccurate. A case can be made that fear has been used successfully as a short-term motivator in many instances. This is especially true if the thing at risk such as a job, health, or family; is of high value and the fearful person sees no other way out.

It can also be said, however, that fear as a leadership approach has a shelf life. That is to say, like food that loses its freshness, over time the approach losses its impact. The value of fear-based leadership declines.

Unfortunately, for those who rely on fear as a leadership tool there is no visible expiration date available. One day the approach may seem to be driving action, increased performance, and unpaid overtime. Then without notice fearful associates decide that something has to give. They do a personal cost-benefit analysis and question if the thing they fear is worse than what they are going through to avoid it.

Over the past 30 years it has been my observation that not only do fears have a shelf life, those shelf lives get shorter and shorter over time when a leader plays the fear card too often. It appears employees, when exposed to fear as the 'go to' leadership strategy, begin to recognize the signs, recover from the fear more quickly, and with increased precision determine whether there is benefit in playing the game.

I would be hard pressed to recall a time when top performance over time was motivated by fear.

Apathy

While teaching at the US Air Force Academy I was assigned to the Behavioral Science department. One of the other Associate Professors was an Army Major who was studying the effects of lesions on the brain impacting dementia. Because my grandfather had been diagnosed with early onset dementia her work fascinated me. It also gave me another perspective on fear.

As she conducted her research she noted the rats in the experiment early on fought or ran to avoid the process. There was no doubt on some level the process of creating the lesions was uncomfortable and possibly painful. At some point in the process the subjects stopped reacting and allowed the researcher to insert the probe.

I wondered if this was a new fear response, Freeze. However, my peer thought it was better described as apathy. She felt at some point in the process they accepted that this was their new life, it was not killing them, and just didn't care anymore. If viewed from a human perspective, they were basically saying 'What's the worst you can do to me? You are already playing with my head every day.'

This holds true with employees whose bosses manipulate them with fear. In the early phases the fear of job loss, public embarrassment, or alienation, can drive an employee to work harder. Over time, however, the impact is diluted. The technique loses its luster and apathy sets in if threats never come to fruition.

Inside jokes (e.g., 'What are they going to do fire us?' or 'That was brutal, but no one died') shared in the leader's absence became a way of expressing apathy regarding the approach. In the long run, fear-based approaches become the leadership equivalent of the boy who cried wolf.

Fait Accompli

The final discussion point looks at how the efficacy of fear-based leadership relies on the belief that no other option exists. Many leaders who consciously use this leadership approach position the threat as a Fait Accompli, a thing that has been decided leaving their employees with no option.

A fait accompli relies on the impacted person believing that the situation actually has no other outcome and the only option is to accept. However, when an individual makes the move from fear response to problem solving, typically options surface. Exploration of options nullifies the fait accompli and dilutes the fear.

For example, the threat of being laid off or fired is only without option if you believe your current job is the only alternative. Countless individuals move from fear of being fired to exploring other job opportunities or retirement. Exploring other opportunities might uncover benefits that your current job does not offer. Questions about retirement might lead you to acknowledge it is actually possible. A job search might allow you to do that thing you have always wanted to do (e.g., teach, fund raise, work for a non-profit). At some point the exploration reduces the fear and clears a path for action.

The end result is dissipation of fear and disqualification of the fait accompli.

Leadership Playbook

Hopefully these tips will help leaders diminish the use of fear-based leadership. For those who use it often I hope this will give you food for thought. For those who find themselves in a fear-based situation I hope this gives you more alternatives to help your employees navigate change and achieve success. For the new, emerging, or aspiring leaders I hope this provides guidance for your future.

Don't

It is probably no surprise that a book about where fear fails takes a stand against fear-based leadership. Students, friends, loved ones, clients, and peers can all attest to the fact I have a healthy dislike for the intentional use of fear as motivator or leadership style. My dislike has deep roots developed over time. It was probably self-evident throughout this chapter.

My advice to leaders and executives I work with is simple: DON'T!

There will be plenty of times when you will have to communicate changes or bad news that will instill fear in the hearts of your employees. In today's challenging, competitive world fear invoking situations abound. There clearly is no reason to create your own or leverage the ones that occur to turn up the heat.

Surely your time, intellect, and experience are better spent removing barriers to success, focusing employees on the task at hand, and problem-solving. Having employees focus and contribute is always preferable to distracting conversations about the 'bullies' they work for.

Hone Your Skills

Today's organizational context has been called a VUCA world, marked by Volatility, Uncertainty, Complexity, and Ambiguity. We are well past 'there is nothing constant but change.' So, while you will be well-served not to use fear intentionally you must hone the skills that will allow you to assist your employees, associates, teams, and other leaders in moving past the fear.

At the top of the list is building expertise in the art of communicating. Clear, concise, and honest communication serves to calm fears and provide direction. Fear of the unknown and uncertainty wane quickly when confronted with information delivered in a clear and powerful way. Take the time to get the messages right and ensure you are well-informed.

Having a well-developed skillset for communicating, addressing, and navigating change (i.e. change leadership) is also an imperative. The elements of VUCA and fear dissipates when confronted with a change strategy devised and implemented by a skilled leader.

In support of change leadership and communication skills, developing your ability to understand, create, and implement strategy is paramount. This skillset requires you to be able to formulate strategy and execute it in a way that guarantees successful results.

Finally, spend as much time honing your EQ (emotional quotient) as your IQ (intelligence quotient). Empathy and understanding are powerful tools in dealing with the effects of fear. Skills to focus on include:

- Correctly identifying emotions

- Understanding the emotions and their impact

- Expressing your understanding

- Managing emotions

Clear the Path

Inextricably linked to fear management and a return to productivity is the concept of removing barriers so your employees can do their best work. If your employees are focused on a lack of resources, then they are not focused on the job itself. If your associates fear bottle necks will cause delays they will be held accountable for, then they are not focused on their deliverables. You get the picture.

Clearing the path can take many forms all aimed at reducing fear or stress and ensuring results are achieved. Here are a few that come to mind:

- Dealing with other functions/departments who create a bottleneck for your operations

- Acquiring the tools/systems/digital resources team members need to do their jobs

- Getting the budget or approval for capital expenditures to upgrade tools making task accomplishment and growth more likely

- Running interference when a client, another function, or senior leadership are looking to blame someone

- Help your team stay focused by dealing directly with rumors, top down communications, and change directives

Clearing the path may be the best way to keep the noise down and fear responses at a manageable level. It will be time well spent.

Chapter 6

How Courage Triumphs

"Success is not final, failure is not fatal: It is the courage to continue that counts."

Winston Churchill

As this book came into focus I began capturing stories and examples of where fear fails. The flip side, stories of how courage triumphed also surfaced and were captured. People, teams, and organizations who pushed through their fears and courageously succeeded where others might have failed.

At some point, it occurred to me that the most appropriate ending for this book is a look at **How Courage Triumphs**. This is the exciting part. Telling the stories of those who conquer fear and do some pretty amazing things.

Let's start with courageous Individuals and their incredible stories.

COURAGEOUS INDIVIDUALS

What You Don't Know Won't Stop You

Recently I attended a three-day author's workshop. For the most part the participants ranged in age from mid-thirties to late sixties. Many of us had carried our unwritten books around in our heads for years. Letting fears of some sort delay us from putting it in print.

The morning of the second day, while waiting to be invited into the workshop, we were milling around in the waiting area. Across the room there was a young girl who clearly did not fit the 35-69-year-old demographic. I would later learn she is 11 years old.

She was engaged in a conversation with other soon to be authors.

One asked, "Why are you here?"

"To learn." She replied.

Another asked "So are you here to learn how to publish a book."

To which the young girl quietly replied, "More."

At this point her father, Don, spoke up and proudly stated that she was already published.

Please let me introduce you to Michelle Longega Wilson.

Michelle is an incredible young person and author. Wise beyond her years, polite, humble, and gracious. Michelle wrote her first book at age 8 and has written two others since. Quite impressive, right?

While interviewing her parents, Don and Sabrina, the story became even more inspiring. Not only did Michelle publish three books before her 11th birthday, she published them in both English and Italian (my guess, inspired by her mother's heritage). Additionally, her books rose to the top of the Amazon Top Seller List for Children's books.

My interview with Don and Sabrina led to an interesting finding about courageous individuals. That fear has no affect if you don't have the fear in the first place. When I asked if Michelle had any trepidation about writing a book her parents laughed.

Imagine, as they described it, one day your eight-year-old daughter comes into the room and announces she is going to write a book. Jumped in, both feet. Michelle made the decision without the fear of the value, interest, or impact on reputation that adult authors struggle with. While those thoughts eventually surfaced, they came late in the process and were quickly shrugged off by Michelle.

Now it is important to note that Michelle was not without fear. The success of her books led to public engagements, opportunities to be interviewed, and speeches. All of which Michelle found a bit daunting.

Once again, however, courage triumphed. She faced her fears and moved forward. Michelle used preparation to mitigate the fear. She wrote out what she wanted to say and practiced it like she would for one of her school plays. Over time it became easier for Michelle, according to Sabrina. My take as an outside observer, Micelle has moved well past any social anxiety she may have had.

There are some confounding variables here that warrant addressing. Yes, Michelle is bright and courageous. And, her parents clearly helped mitigate her fear before it occurred. In the brief time spent with Don and Sabrina, it was apparent that they are involved, proud, and encouraging. Although they may have been shocked by Michelle's proclamation that she was going to write a book they avoided planting and growing fears.

Needless-to-say, a fear unrecognized has little to no impact. If we can muster up the strength to ignore or not attend to a fear it clearly loses its ability to drive our actions and behaviors.

In this case, and many others, what you don't know won't stop you or have power over you.

They Make the Call

Many of us were glued to the TV after the Boston Marathon bombings as authorities looked for the brothers who perpetrated the heinous act. At some point during our vigil breaking news notified us that one of the brothers had been captured. He was injured and hiding in a boat in someone's back yard.

In a world where many look the other way or chose not to get involved, the owner of the home did the opposite. Having noticed that there was something awry with the boat stored in his yard, he immediately called the police setting the response and capture in motion.

Those who push through the fear. Who take the courageous path. Who have a positive impact; make the call, say something, get personally involved. For them there are no red carpets, photo shoots, parades, or huge salaries for playing a game. They are everyday heroes who make all of the difference in our world.

On a daily basis individuals fight fear responses to do the right thing. Instead of running, hiding, or freezing; they confront their fears and stand up for a cause, a person, or core values. Sometimes fear is the door we have to pass through to achieve success and do the right thing.

Making the call, saying something, or taking action when others are frozen is rarely easy. Being an everyday hero never is. The choice is ours. When tested courage beckons us to make the call.

Face Fear Head On

While working for a small graphic design firm I met a talented graphic designer, Chris Francisco. Chris is one of those individuals who lights up a room and becomes a quick friend. He is talented, charming, full of life and optimism.

There came a time in our friendship when Chris missed several days of work and was not his vivacious self when he returned. He worked at being himself, but there was an underlying sadness or worry that was out of the norm for him.

I soon learned the baby he and his wife were expecting, had been born prematurely and was courageously fighting for his life. His fight was nothing short of heroic.

Please allow me to introduce you to this young hero, Apollo-Max Mandap Francisco (aka Baby Lucky).

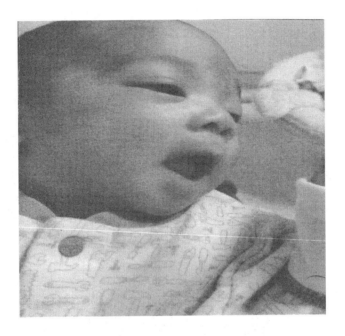

Apollo-Max was born on March 8, 2010 and
weighed 3 pounds, 8 ounces.

Chris noted that while adults were overwhelmed by their fear, their son was fighting for his life and was the most courageous person he had ever witnessed. Apollo-Max hung onto life with all his might, spirit, and will. In the process, he taught us all some of life's most important lessons.

We celebrated Baby Lucky's life on May 12, 2010. I have carried the card from his life celebration with me for the past 7 years. I think Chris and Roella's words best describe his courage and impact on those he met:

Some of us take a lifetime to learn the fundamentals of life & true love. Our family was blessed to obtain this knowledge through a young man who weighed only 5 lbs. 10 oz. but had the strength of a warrior and a heart of gold. We will miss you our Rising Son as your journey will remind us how to live life with pure love. You touched many souls, while coming in touch with only a few. There won't be a day gone by, that we as a family will not miss you. Thank you for touching our life Son. We'll see you again.

From my vantage point Apollo-Max successfully taught his family how to push through scary challenges and charge ahead with courage. It was in evidence as his parents courageously celebrated his life on that day in May. It continues to show as they keep his short life and story alive daily.

By extension, those of us who know Baby Lucky's parents are touched by his story. We gain clarity about what facing fear head on looks like.

Never Quit

At age 85, Rainer Weiss was notified that he and two other physicists had been awarded the Nobel Prize in Physics. Quite the accomplishment. To work your whole life trying to prove Einstein was correct. To finally have your life's work, with the discovery of gravitational waves, prove Einstein's prediction of ripples in space time.

However, while this accomplishment supports the concept of never quit it is only part of the story.

Dr. Weiss had to overcome failure early in life to travel his incredible journey. He accomplished something that many have tried and only a select few have accomplished. He applied to and was accepted to attend Massachusetts Institute of Technology (MIT).

Unfortunately, he had difficulties early on and flunked out of MIT. Can you imagine? Achieving your goal of going to MIT only to flunk out. What would a young person do facing such a daunting situation? How would you explain this to friends and family? Do you run away or hide in place?

For Rainer Weiss, courage dictated finding a different path and never giving up. Without the requirement of class or study, he decided to work as an electronics technician in a MIT lab. He learned as much as he could while working as a tech. He also overcame his social anxiety.

His hard work paid off. He eventually returned to school at MIT received a Bachelor's degree and eventually his PhD. Later he became a professor at the school where his journey began.

When he addressed the media, his humility was overwhelming. He clearly was thinking about his initial failure, a failure that was overcome by his drive (and courage) to never ever quit.

COURAGEOUS TEAMS

You will recall, our review of fears at the team level encompassed the concept of Groupthink and fears regarding public embarrassment, conflict, and being ostracized. Successful teams engage in behaviors and activities that counteract these fears. Here are some examples.

Leverage Strengths

Have you ever been on a team that performed at the highest level? A team of people who you might never have imagined working together because they were so diverse and yet, somehow, they just worked.

The foodies among you probably are familiar with a show on the Food Network, The Kitchen. The cast is made up of:

Jeff Mauro, a charismatic, folksy personality who gives the show a comfortable and humorous feel.

Sunny Anderson, an Air Force veteran who is personality plus, witty, and brings southern, down-home cooking to the show.

Geoffrey Zakarian, a somewhat stoic chef with phenomenal skills and a formal, upscale approach to his recipes and suggestions.

Katie Lee, charming and a bit more measured that Jeff or Sunny, Katie focuses on making cooking fun and simple, presenting recipes that are quick, easy, interesting, and delicious.

Marcela Valladolid, open and approachable Marcela provides family recipes with a Latin flare, handed down from generation to generation. Her focus on family brings a warmth to the show.

The hosts are an eclectic combination of talent, formal and informal training, and distinctive personalities. The magic occurs in the leveraging of each of their strengths and personalities. They tease, support, add to, and praise each other in an authentic way that makes the show interesting and very successful.

The Kitchen is a positive model of what complimentary diversity looks like. Their seamless handoffs, inclusive approach, and respect for each other commands the audience's attention and makes for great TV. The result is a powerful team achieving results (i.e. high ratings, great informative entertainment).

This is never more evident than when a guest host joins the show or one of the cast members is absent. The show remains informative and interesting but it is clear something is missing. The chemistry is just different.

Having the courage to let each team member contribute their unique talents in their own way is a recipe for success (pun intended). When it works, a team will be at the top of their game and deliver superior results. Team members will feel included, valued, and engaged. They are not afraid of contributing, embarrassment, or alienation.

Team leaders who encourage healthy competition, full engagement, and contribution by all team members tend to produce results exceeding expectations. The members of the team will contribute time, energy, and creativity. Conflict will be minimal and quickly handled because the leader and team members respect each other and know the whole will always produce more than the sum of the parts.

Create a Context for Contribution

Our neighborhood has seen an influx of new neighbors from India in the past five years. Our new neighbors have quickly become an integral part of our community. They are friendly, family oriented, and openly share their cultural traditions while working hard to assimilate into American culture. This has been reinforced over the past couple of years when Diwali lights go up each fall and a month or so later are joined by ghosts, witches, and jack-o-lanterns for Halloween.

Recently, while walking Maddie, I came upon a group of women gathered around one of the park benches in the neighborhood. They were ten or twelve strong and from my perspective at least 8 of them were speaking at the same time. At the center of the activity was a young woman sitting on the bench.

This ad hoc Wedding Planning Committee was in full swing, the participants talking over each other with excitement and creativity in abundance. Clearly there were no concerns over hurt feelings, presenting a bad idea, or being ignored. In unison contributions went on for several minutes. I wondered if any of the ideas would ever be captured and implemented.

Then something incredible happened. The chatter subsided and the women began speaking one at a time, brainstorming and building on each idea. Within minutes they had chosen locations for both the wedding and reception, who would do what on the day of the wedding from helping the bride get ready to making the guests feel welcome. They even outlined the bride and grooms' departure and where they would honeymoon. It was a sight to see and so instructive.

Imagine what a team could accomplish if they created a similar, safe environment for providing inputs and brainstorming. Could the process of generating ideas, solving problems, and making decisions be as successful as this planning committee?

Team leaders who encourage input, minimize criticism of ideas during the incubation process, and ensure each idea is used to create the best solution, will build team cohesion and breed success.

Associates who feel free to contribute without ridicule, retribution, or embarrassment will produce countless quality ideas and results. Achieving successful outcomes is commonplace for teams that effortlessly generate ideas, feel included, and have a safe place to do so. The process and end results can be as easily obtained as those achieved by the Wedding Planning Committee.

Run Toward as Others Run Away

Twenty-four, seven, fifty-two men and women we don't know and rarely engage are working to protect us or save our lives. Every day firefighters, police officers, and emergency medical professionals are on shift just in case we need them for safety or survival.

These incredible teams run in the direction of the fire or the sound of the gunshot while others run in the opposite direction. Our recent history includes countless examples of their willingness to confront fear while others cowered.

These heroes ran into burning towers giving their lives to save countless others. We have seen others place themselves in harm's way to protect those who were protesting against them when a madman started shooting without cause or provocation. On local nightly news broadcasts, there are myriad examples of off-duty firefighters or police officers pulling people from burning cars, catching babies tossed from a burning building, or saving someone who has fallen through broken ice.

They perform CPR, deliver babies, and help those who are lost and disoriented. These professionals are at their very best when tragedy strikes. They brave storms, forest fires, floods, and earthquakes while others are paralyzed with fear. Teams of first responders perform miracles daily.

While these teams may seem superhuman or peerless, their success actually can inform teams who are called to a different type of heroics. Teams called upon to create innovations that simplify our lives, advance medicines that will extend our longevity and cure our ills, or provide services to help us live more comfortably from 1 to 102.

Replicating the first responder's success follows a simple formula. First, you must muster up courage to move forward when your competitors and rivals are frozen in fear. Second, use your preparation, skills and innate talents to push through fear when it arises.

Third, squelch doubts or crises of faith and move forward with the full knowledge you are ready and prepared to navigate the change or challenge facing you and your team. Fourth, celebrate courage and capture the gain (i.e., document what went well and actions taken). Fifth and finally; refuel, repack, recover, and prepare for the next challenge.

Courageous teams are not an anomaly. Success can be achieved by creating a context for contribution, ensuring everyone is fully engaged, and pushing through team fears because you are fully prepared, well trained, and confident in your actions because the team is up to the task at hand.

COURAGEOUS ORGANIZATIONS

A CEO I respect greatly once told me all he wanted from those in his organization was their best effort, to be fully accountable for their commitments, and to achieve organizational goals in a way that would not look bad on the front page of the Wall Street Journal.

The impetus to perform as a courageous organization is pretty simple. When all is said, those who lead and work for complex entities want to be proud of what they do, the impact of their work, and how the work is accomplished. We established earlier how fear puts organizations at risk. Fear of attack, obsolescence, and loss drive behaviors that are incongruent with the good conduct of an enterprise.

Additionally, we discussed how fear-based leadership leads to dysfunction, mistrust, and a context for unethical behavior. All in contrast to the CEO's statement above.

Whether intentional or not, when those in power use some fairly common phrases they are creating a context for unethical behavior. Here are few that come quickly to mind:

"Do whatever it takes."

"Do it or else."

"Just make it happen."

"Failure is not an option."

The good news is that there is a better way. Let's look at how Courageous Organizations change the game and win.

Be True to Your Values and Culture

The business landscape is littered with organizations who altered or moved away from their core values and/or culture and failed. As discussed earlier this sometimes occurs when two organizations merge. Sometimes market pressures lead to abandonment of values and culture.

Successful organizations find the courage to either inoculate themselves from ever violating their values or create a culture so strong that they always find their way back should they stray.

One organization that comes to mind is Johnson & Johnson. In 1982 the company faced a major crisis. In September of that year seven people in Chicago died after taking Tylenol. It was determined the Tylenol capsules consumed by these victims were laced with cyanide. Tylenol was Johnson & Johnson's best-selling product at the time.

Over the years, we have heard horror stories about organizations who struggled with difficult situations and decisions linked to such crises. Often the story notes discussion of losses, cost-benefit analysis, and the potential extent of the damage.

Johnson & Johnson was different. It placed its consumers first and immediately recalled 31 million bottles of Tylenol. Many pundits and analyst predicted that the Tylenol brand, which accounted for at least 17% of the company's net income, would never recover. The prediction missed the mark.

Two months after the crisis, Johnson & Johnson introduced new Tylenol with tamper proof caps. Although their market share had dropped to 7% in this market, shortly after the introduction of the new Tylenol packaging they had moved back to a position of 30% market share.

So, why did this turn out so well for Johnson & Johnson?

Johnson & Johnson, under the leadership of their Chairman, James Burke, did the right thing and did it without hesitation. This was made possible because Johnson & Johnson had decided long before this incident that they would do no harm and that they would take immediate action should one of their products do so. It was clearly stated in their corporate values and procedures were put in place to react quickly should the need arise. There was no room for debating profit, alternatives, or doing a risk analysis. The decision was made well before it was tested in 1982. Decisions made before a crisis are typically better than those made in the heat of the moment.

Courageous organizations are values based. They have the courage to set high standards for themselves and live up to those standards when trying times or situations occur. In the case of Johnson & Johnson, they took a situation that represented a violation of trust with their customers and turned it into a trust building event. To this day they remain one of the most trusted companies in the world.

Create a Context for Innovation and Success

It has been said that the greatest thing a company can do for customers, the community they belong to, and their employees is to remain a going concern.

In today's nanosecond world staying in business is more complex than ever. The era, if it ever really existed, where a company could establish a product or service, build a brand, and just keep selling more of the same is long gone. Markets change quickly, new entrants join the fray daily, and new technologies change the game often. Combine this with an increasingly more demanding consumer and it's tough going for those who can't innovate and remain agile.

Living in Cupertino, California I have long had an interest in Apple and how it goes about its business. Through the years many things have changed and yet Apple has continued to compete and perform well.

One thing that has led to Apple's success and longevity, is that Apple established it's 'Why' a long time ago and it's 'Why' is the lens through which they view business and operational decisions. The ultimate purpose, their 'Why' is to makes people's lives easier.

It started with an interface that was mouse driven and much more intuitive than other computers at the time. Apple migrated to helping people carry 10,000 tunes in their pocket, then easy to use smartphones, and a tablet that people actually purchased and used.

So, at the core is the simple 'Why.' However, without innovation, their "Why" would be limited to an old definition of making life easier and their products and solutions would become passé. Some have said this was the source of conflict between John Scully and Steve Jobs. While Apple achieved incredible revenue growth during Mr. Scully's tenure, his approach was borne of his time at PepsiCo and steeped in growing market share by selling more of Apple's core products instead of using innovation to create new markets.

With Scully's departure and Jobs' return Apple shifted quickly back to its prior focus on innovation as the means to make people's lives easier. They also honored their "Why" by shifting their position on proprietary software on their computers. They even partnered with former competitors, in an attempt to make life easier for their dedicated Mac fans.

Recently I overheard a conversation that reinforced the necessity for courageous organizations to innovate constantly in today's warp speed world. While waiting for a flight, I overheard three passengers discussing a new version of a popular smartphone. Their analysis: "It's the same old suit with new shoes." They clearly were not impressed. In that moment, it hit me that the iPhone was celebrating its ten-year anniversary. It seems like it has been around for much longer. It also occurred to me that when President Obama was elected the first time the iPad had not even been invented yet. Apple has introduced five generations of the iPad since that time.

Courageous organizations innovate, change, and succeed. They innovate to remain relevant. They innovate because the world and their consumers are changing dramatically in very short order. They innovate because it is the antiviral for the fear of obsolescence, loss, and extinction. The option is to become commoditized, compete based solely on price, and eventually disappear.

Leaders who create a context for innovation engage their organizations and their key stakeholders in activities that move their organizations forward instead of fear responses and behaviors that ultimately guarantee the company's demise.

Seek Input from Your Key Stakeholders

We discussed earlier how the fear of loss (Key Customer or Top Employee) can paralyze a company. It is perplexing that a company in trouble would not seek the inputs of the very clients and employees they worry about losing. As if going out of business is better than hearing tough feedback from those who have the greatest impact on your success or failure.

Almost 20 years ago Tom Peters (author of In Search of Excellence, Passion for Excellence, and the Pursuit of Wow) chronicled probably one of the greatest examples of a turnaround linked directly to receiving key stakeholder feedback. Dr. Peters highlighted the near extinction of America's last motorcycle company, Harley-Davidson. As the story goes Vaughn Beals, Harley-Davidson's CEO, inherited a company in deep trouble.

At the time, early 1980s, Harley Davidson had earned a reputation for a shoddy product and poor workmanship. Motorcycles on showroom floors had cardboard under 'new' motorcycles because they were leaking oil. A once loyal client base was quickly losing faith in the brand.

Mr. Beals tried countless maneuvers to turn things around, impact the quality of their motorcycles, and improve their reputation in the marketplace.

Needless-to-say, the employees building the motorcycles had long lost pride in what they produced. Salespeople were less than enthusiastic promoting Harleys that were subpar. The brand was not only struggling in the marketplace but inside the organization as well.

If memory serves, Vaughn Beals at some point decided that he had tried everything he could think of to change the dire situation Harley-Davidson was in. He was completely out of ideas.

In this time of desperation, Mr. Beals actually came up with the one approach that would make all of the difference. He decided to seek inputs from two very important constituencies.

Beals decided to spend more time on the factory floor. He walked around and spoke with associates. He started holding skip level meetings to get unfiltered feedback. The information proved invaluable. Employees who wanted to be proud of what they made had clearly been thinking about what was wrong on the shop floor. Once they were given an opportunity to speak freely they shared all of their concerns and frustrations.

One of the key outcomes of this information sharing was a major change to how parts made their way to the floor for assembly. In the past, parts were delivered to the floor in batches. If a part had a problem or defect it was likely that the entire rack would also be faulty. Eventually assemblers just gave up trying to influence the process and put the defective parts on the motorcycles.

Based on this feedback the company retooled their assembly line. Parts are delivered through an elaborate overhead system as needed for assembly. At any point assemblers can halt the process by pushing a button to alert the fabricators that a problem exists. This one change required an initial capital investment that paid huge dividends. Quality improved and employees regained pride in the work they were doing.

Concurrent with seeking employee input Mr. Beals also sought the input of another very important group, Harley's loyal customers. Seeking a venue to get customer feedback, Mr. Beals created Harley Owners Groups (HOGs). He invited loyal customers (fans) to HOGs and rode with them. He listened actively and asked lots of questions. Once the door was opened, feedback came from around the world. At first, the feedback referenced all that was wrong with the company and its products. However, in very short order criticism shifted to thanks for listening and praise for improvements in quality.

Rumors of Harley-Davidson's demise were premature. Feedback from key constituencies saved this American icon. A CEO's desperation led him to courageously seek the inputs that saved the company.

This is just one approach, not the approach. Your organization may have the need to seek information from completely different sources. The real question is whether you have been seeking input from those who could impact your organization in very positive ways?

Here are some sources of feedback that might benefit your organization:

- Faced with a downturn in employee productivity use an employee engagement survey to get at the potential source.

- A leadership performance gap might warrant seeking feedback from multiple sources (peers, employees, and boss) to highlight strengths to leverage and areas needing development.

- Difficulty wooing the best and brightest might warrant a look at your organizations 'interviews' tab on glassdoor.com.

- Loss of business, especially long-term clients, might warrant viewing Yelp! Reviews and creating a strategy for responding and/or seeking more information. Client surveys generated directly from your organization might also make sense.

- Engaging future employees using focus groups. This is more than attending college fairs. Run focus groups or surveys to get their feedback on what they are looking for in an employer.

- Structured interviews conducted by behavioral science professionals in a work unit that has more than normal disruptions and conflict.

The key is to make sure you have the best information to make the best decisions impacting your organization, your employees, and those who use your products and services.

As noted earlier, this book has been several years in the making. The journey has been laced and influenced by countless situations exposing fears, failures, abandoned dreams, and loss. Fear on many occasions led to disappointing outcomes for individuals, teams, and organizations.

The journey also included myriad examples of how courage triumphs. Ordinary people, groups, and entities who found the courage to push through fearful situations. In most cases, they arrived on the other side of fear with pride, success, and support. When they fell short, typically their new-found courage gave impetus to picking themselves up, dusting themselves off, and trying again. Like the stairs to the Citadel in Quebec, once you face a fear it loses its hold on you.

MY HOPE IS THAT YOU CONFRONT AND CONQUER YOUR FEARS AND EMBRACE YOUR COURAGEOUS TRIUMPHS

How Courage Triumphs

is in the works!

If you would like to have your story of courage and triumph included in the book, please send it to:

bruce@bgoeasenterprises.com

ACKNOWLEDGEMENTS

First and foremost, I would like to thank my wife, Christina, for listening to my rants about fear and its negative impact for years. Her support for the past 40 years has been my lifeblood and allowed me to take risk and display courage knowing unconditional love was always nearby.

Special thanks to Chris and Roella Francisco for allowing me share Apollo-Max's story of courage. I am humbled to have the opportunity to ensure his young spirit, filled with love and courage is captured for all time.

Also, special thanks to Don, Sabrina, and Michelle Longega Wilson for allowing me to share Michelle's wonderful story. Finishing the book became easier, and without excuses, after meeting this incredible young author.

Finally, Thank You Mom and Dad! You taught us how to believe in ourselves, to never abandon our values, to fight for the underdog, and to face our fears head on. Even in your final days you each taught us how to face fear with grace and courage. Love you both more than words can describe.

Made in the USA
Middletown, DE
21 January 2018